To Henry Ley

PRELUDE AND FUGUE IN C MINOR
I PRELUDE

R. VAUGHAN WILLIAMS

© Oxford University Press 1930

Printed in Great Britain

OXFORD UNIVERSITY PRESS, MUSIC DEPARTMENT, GREAT CLARENDON STREET, OXFORD OX2 6DP
The Moral Rights of the Composer have been asserted. Photocopying this copyright material is ILLEGAL.

The orchestral material (score and parts) is available on hire.

ff
Gt. to 15th. (with 16ft.) coupled to full Sw.

Sept. 2nd 1921
Revised July 29th 1923 and March 6th 1930

II FUGUE

add Full Sw.

Ossia

Reduce to   Gt. soft 8 & 4 ft. coupled to Sw. 16, 8, 4 ft.

Aug. 23rd 1921
Revised July 30th 1923 and March 6th 1930
OXFORD UNIVERSITY PRESS